The Woman
The Warrior

Equipped for purpose and empowered for destiny

J. Benjamin

ISBN 979-8-89043-616-0 (paperback)
ISBN 979-8-89043-617-7 (digital)

Christian Faith Publishing
832 Park Avenue
Meadville, PA 16335
www.christianfaithpublishing.com

Printed in the United States of America

Introduction

I was prompted to write this book, encouraged by a good friend of mine one winter evening in December 2020 as I found myself preaching to him while he remained utterly silent.

Every woman needs to know who she is and what she represents. A lack of an understanding of purpose may lead to a detour on the journey of one's life.

It is important that every woman asks pertinent questions as she begins her journey for a purpose- and God-driven life.

Who am I? What role am I called to play? How do I go about it?

It is unfortunate that some of our parents never teach us some grounding principles, perhaps because of a lack of knowledge themselves. While I will take no credit away from those parents who taught and groomed their daughters to become good, loving, supportive wives and homemakers, unfortunately, there is a vast number of women who did not have the opportunity to have that guidance and basically learned from what they saw their mothers do while adopting the same ideology, an ideology that is passed from generation to generation but may remain devoid of the light of God's purpose and enriched with worldly understanding.

Every woman has been called to be more than she thinks she is but is limited by what she doesn't know.

A woman who understands her role and confronts her battles is a woman who is set for greatness and prepared for the journey to be a godly wife.

Show me a woman who has fought the battle and prevailed, and I will show you a woman of destiny, a great woman who understands her role and is fully equipped for the journey as a wife from God.

It is not unusual that several women may get caught up in an unreal fantasy made up of emotions, attraction, sentiments, and tradition and constrained by the lack of the original perspective.

I think it is imperative to set the foundation by understanding the inner workings of the dynamic that occurred from the beginning of time.

I acknowledge that not every woman chooses or is desirous of marriage. Nevertheless, whether single or married, the value and role a woman plays in humanity should never be underestimated.

C h a p t e r   1

Foundational Dynamic from the Beginning of Time

There are some truths that are clearly inscribed in the Word of God that need to be understood for us to avail ourselves of a better insight.

> In the beginning God created the heaven and the earth. And the earth was without form, and void; and darkness was upon the face of the deep. And the Spirit of God moved upon the face of the waters. And God said, Let there be light: and there was light. And God saw the light, that it was good: and God divided the light from the darkness. And God called the light Day, and the darkness he called Night. And the evening and the morning were the first day. (Genesis 1:1–5)

In the book of Genesis 1:1–5, you will notice that verses 3–4 say, "God said, 'Let there be light' and there was light. And God saw the light."

You will notice that God spoke before he saw, so whatever you wish to see materialize in your life must be spoken prior to visualizing it.

I have deliberately reviewed and stated this because this will be your guiding principle as you journey in the freeway of life.

> And God said, Let us make man in our image, after our likeness: and let them have dominion over the fish of the sea, and over the fowl of the air, and over the cattle, and over all the earth, and over every creeping thing that creepeth upon the earth. (Genesis 1:26)

In Genesis 1:26, it is said man was made in the image of God and his likeness and given dominion over everything on earth. He was in charge and given purpose.

One of the purposes of man was also to ensure that God's creations on earth were managed and sustained. This is better exemplified in Genesis 2:4–7.

> These are the generations of the heavens and of the earth when they were created, in the day that the Lord God made the earth and the heavens, and every plant of the field before it was in the earth, and every herb of the field before it grew: for the

Lord God had not caused it to rain upon the earth, and there was not a man to till the ground. But there went up a mist from the earth, and watered the whole face of the ground. And the Lord God formed man of the dust of the ground, and breathed into his nostrils the breath of life; and man became a living soul. (Genesis 2:4–7)

In verse 5, there was no man to till the ground, but a mist went up from the earth and watered the whole face of the ground.

The good thing about God is that he put systems in place to enable man to function optimally where he placed him.

And the Lord God planted a garden eastward in Eden; and there he put the man whom he had formed. And out of the ground made the Lord God to grow every tree that is pleasant to the sight, and good for food; the tree of life also in the midst of the garden, and the tree of knowledge of good and evil. And a river went out of Eden to water the garden; and from thence it was parted, and became into four heads. The name of the first is Pishon: that is it which compasseth the whole land of Havilah, where there is gold; and the gold of that land is good: there is bdellium and the onyx stone. And the name of the second river is Gihon: the same is it that compasseth the whole land of Ethiopia. And the name of the third river is Hiddekel: that is it which goeth toward the east of Assyria. And the fourth river is Euphrates. And the Lord God took the man, and put him into the garden of Eden to dress it and to keep it. And the Lord God commanded the man, saying, Of every tree of the garden thou mayest freely eat: But of the tree of the knowledge of good and evil, thou shalt not eat of it: for in the day that thou eatest thereof thou shalt surely die. (Genesis 2:8–17)

In Genesis 2:8–17, it is said man had purpose and was focused on doing God's will. At this time, man was positioned in a certain locality by God and asked to tend and keep the garden.

Man flourished as even the river that came out of Eden to water the garden had four riverheads. The first riverhead was called Pishon and skirted the whole land of Havilah, where there was good gold. Furthermore, bdellium (incense) and onyx stone were there.

Man had an abundance of food as God had made every tree that is pleasant to the sight and good for food grow.

Man was given direction and instructions, one of which was that of every tree in the garden, he may freely eat, but of the tree of knowledge of good and evil "you shall not eat, for in the day that you eat of it you shall surely die."

Man lived a purpose-driven life within the confines of the directive given by his maker and creator.

Chapter 2

The Helper

The Role from a Godly Perspective

> And the Lord God said, It is not good that the man should be alone; I will make him an help meet for him. And out of the ground the Lord God formed every beast of the field, and every fowl of the air; and brought them unto Adam to see what he would call them: and whatsoever Adam called every living creature, that was the name thereof. And Adam gave names to all cattle, and to the fowl of the air, and to every beast of the field; but for Adam there was not found an help meet for him. (Genesis 2:18–20)

What is a helper, and who is the person that qualifies to be a helper?

A helper is a person who helps someone else. A person who is a helper has certain characteristics that include being genuinely caring, having a calm manner, being highly dependable and honest, to mention a few.

A comparable helper could not be found, though, for the man that named every animal that the Lord brought to him. The animals and creatures were formed from the ground by God, yet not one was found to be comparable to him. Otherwise, they would have been well suited for the man. Simply put, none of the animals were found to be similar to him.

This created a dilemma, and the approach God took was reflective of his wisdom and powers. As you may recall, in Genesis 2:7, God made man from the dust of the ground and breathed into his nostril the breath of life (*zoe* in Greek), then the man became a living being. To get man in the image and likeness of God, something came out of God into man; so to get a helper comparable to man, something had to come out of man to make the woman as the breath of life from God flowed in him.

The helper that a man needs to fulfill his God given purpose is in the mind of God, and every man needs to tap into it. God moved in Adam's life for his benefit without his help or interference as long as he was within the center of God's will.

There are things about each man who remain in the center of God's will that even before they ask, he has already gone ahead of them as he is mindful of those in his will.

The only other time the significance of the word *helper* was used was in John 15:26–27: "But when the Helper comes, whom I shall send to you from the Father, the Spirit of truth who proceeds from the Father, He will testify of Me. And you also will bear witness, because you have been with Me from the beginning."

The word *helper* here refers to the Spirit of truth, the Holy Spirit. The Holy Spirit helps and guides you. God is very particular about the helpers he provides, and we need to be careful with how we engage with the helper.

> Wherefore I say unto you, All manner of sin and blasphemy shall be forgiven unto men: but the blasphemy against the Holy Ghost shall not be forgiven unto men. And whosoever speaketh a word against the Son of man, it shall be forgiven him: but whosoever speaketh against the Holy Ghost, it shall not be forgiven him, neither in this world, neither in the world to come. (Mathew 12:31–32)

In Mathew 12:31–32, if you disregard or disdain the helper sent by God in the person of the Holy Spirit, there will be negative consequences.

Similarly, when God sends a man a helper, he expects that they should be related to with gentleness and an understanding that he brought them into a man's life for a purpose and, ultimately, to achieve destiny. Hence, he says in 1 Peter 3:7, "Likewise, ye husbands, dwell with them according to knowledge, giving honour unto the wife, as unto the weaker vessel, and as being heirs together of the grace of life; that your prayers be not hindered."

If you maltreat the helper sent by God in the person of your wife, there will be negative consequences too.

If we understand this about God sending us helpers, we need to be very careful about how we relate with these helpers.

A wife who maintains her role as a helper ordained by God and administers her purpose with focus certainly has the backing of God himself.

> And the Lord God caused a deep sleep to fall upon Adam, and he slept: and he took one of his ribs, and closed up the flesh instead thereof; and the rib, which the Lord God had taken from man, made he a woman, and brought her unto the man. And Adam said, This is now bone of my bones, and flesh of my flesh: she shall be called Woman, because she was taken out of Man. (Genesis 2:21–23)

In Genesis 2:21–23, God caused Adam to fall into a deep sleep and removed a rib from him. There was a he before there was a she. Without him, there would've been no her, which means there was a connection that should have been inseparable. The woman was an extension of the life that flowed out of man.

The woman was brought to the man, not the man to the woman. Here you can see that she was supposed to be a blessing from God to him. The introduction of the woman to man was the beginning of a new era, all divinely orchestrated. A man who understands the blessing of a woman from God will be protective and loving toward this God-given helper.

While he was tending to the garden and focused on the tasks God had given him, God was busy taking care of she who would be of benefit to him.

The man said, "This is now the bone of my bone and the flesh of my flesh," and he called her woman because she was taken out of him (Genesis 2:23).

If one is of similar flesh and bone as another, then an attack on the other is ultimately an attack on oneself. An attack can come in diverse ways; it could be degradation, abuse, insults, and rejection. It is highly unlikely that anyone will deliberately abuse themself while knowing that the outcome will be unpleasant.

Unfortunately, in the heat of life and challenges of relationships, we are often caught up in the now and lose sight of the thereafter. The depth of the connection between the man and the woman is hardly emphasized on, and this is largely due to foundational gaps in the understanding of the original dynamic.

In Genesis 2:25 ("And they were both naked, the man and his wife, and were not ashamed"), a man and a woman in their purest form, under the covering of God's auspicious canopy, did not see themselves as naked and were not ashamed.

The accusatory faults that so engulf man and woman in modern-day society was not seen in the perfect makeup of God's creation. They could not see faults or imperfections; as far as they were concerned, all was well, and there was contentment and satisfaction.

The woman had the only man she ever knew, and the man had the only woman he ever knew. And both had a God who loved and was mindful of them.

The complex of inferiority or superiority was not an issue as they operated with oneness of mind and spirit, allowing for an overflow of peace, harmony, and love.

The man worked by tending and keeping the garden, as the Lord had commanded; and he was helped by his helper, the woman. She was there for him. Her presence reminded him that if he was ever weary, she was there. If he needed comforting, she was there for him. If he ever felt lonely, her warm embrace was always there to remind him of the deep unity they had. It was the perfect life balanced by an honest, genuinely caring person who was God-given—the woman.

C h a p t e r   3

Who Am I, and What Is My Role as a Woman?

Now the serpent was more cunning than any beast of the field which the Lord God had made. And he said to the woman, "Has God indeed said, 'You shall not eat of every tree of the garden'?" And the woman said to the serpent, "We may eat the fruit of the trees of the garden; but of the fruit of the tree which is in the midst of the garden, God has said, 'You shall not eat it, nor shall you touch it, lest you die.'" Then the serpent said to the woman, "You will not surely die. For God knows that in the day you eat of it your eyes will be opened, and you will be like God, knowing good and evil." (Genesis 3:1–5)

It is imperative at this juncture to specify who the serpent is. Revelation 20:22 says, "He seized the dragon, that ancient *serpent*, who is the devil, or Satan, and bound him for a thousand years" (emphasis added).

So we understand that the serpent is the devil, or Satan.

Woman of God, who are you listening to? Who do you allow to speak in your life? What are you exposed to? What do you spend your time doing? What are you listening to? Who are your friends? Do your friends point you to the Word?

You do not converse with the devil or aliens. Any narrative, regardless of the source, that does not align with the Word of God on that matter is not of God and should be rejected.

You should be wary of arguments that question the Word of God or give reasons to circumvent the truth or godly instructions to suit your intended actions.

When you entertain a conversation that questions God's authority and Word, you simply put yourself and your family at risk.

> And when the woman saw that the tree was good for food, and that it was pleasant to the eyes, and a tree to be desired to make one wise, she took of the fruit thereof, and did eat, and gave also unto her husband with her; and he did eat. And the eyes of them both were opened, and they knew that they were naked; and they sewed fig leaves together, and made themselves aprons. And they heard the voice of the Lord God walking in the garden in the cool of the day: and Adam and his wife

hid themselves from the presence of the Lord God amongst the trees of the garden. And the Lord God called unto Adam, and said unto him, Where art thou? And he said, I heard thy voice in the garden, and I was afraid, because I was naked; and I hid myself. And he said, Who told thee that thou wast naked? Hast thou eaten of the tree, whereof I commanded thee that thou shouldest not eat? And the man said, The woman whom thou gavest to be with me, she gave me of the tree, and I did eat. And the Lord God said unto the woman, What is this that thou hast done? And the woman said, The serpent beguiled (beguiled could also mean: deceive, mislead or bewitch) me, and I did eat. And the Lord God said unto the serpent, Because thou hast done this, thou art cursed above all cattle, and above every beast of the field; upon thy belly shalt thou go, and dust shalt thou eat all the days of thy life. (Genesis 3:6–14)

In Genesis 3:6–14, she saw that it looked good and pleasant on the outside and that it was desirable to be wise. She thought, *Why not? What about me? Why shouldn't I?* Now she entertained pride, wanting the accolades of importance, while disobeying God. This was driven by her sensuality and not spirituality, and she forgot for a moment whose she was and her purpose.

She took of the fruit and ate it. She also gave it to her husband, and he ate. We now see an interruption of the life God had intended. The one who was made to help now became the one who facilitated the beginning of a new dawn in complete disregard to God.

This changed the trajectory that God had originally intended. There was an unholy alliance between the woman and the deceiver, a partnership that was purposefully targeted. Have you ever wondered why the serpent (the devil) chose and approached the woman? He knew that the woman was the incubator for life and the channel for the outpouring of destines.

> Pride goes before destruction, and
> a haughty spirit before a fall. (Proverbs
> 16:18)

Indeed, we now begin to see the fall of man, who was made in the likeness of God, by the elements of pride.

They hid from God. There was a shame and nakedness they experienced as they wallowed in a sinful nature against God. They had damaged the perfect dynamic of openness, transparency, truth, and righteousness with a righteous God. The relationship was fractured, and the oneness they once enjoyed had been impacted and distorted.

> Then the Lord God called to Adam
> and said to him, "Where are you?"
> (Genesis 3:9)

God called to Adam and not Eve, "Where are you? You are the person I put in charge of the affairs of this garden. I entrusted you to tend to and take care of it… Where are you? You are responsible for what happens down here. Where are you?

"You were not afraid when you named animals that could kill you. You were not afraid when you were on your own. You never even saw your nakedness. But the wedge of sin and disobedience now makes you afraid and exposes you, and now you hide from my presence."

> Then the man said, "The woman whom You gave to be with me, she gave me of the tree, and I ate." And the Lord God said to the woman, "What is this you have done?" The woman said, "The serpent deceived me, and I ate." (Genesis 3:12–13)

"What you have done is far more serious than you think. You have started a new world order. I did not give any instruction to the serpent who you say deceived you. You were instructed, and I conveyed your purposes. Why did you think it was okay to listen to a source other than me? What is this you have done?"

A woman is a gatekeeper. You can choose what you allow to infiltrate your home while your husband is busy, focused on building and fulfilling that which he was called to do.

A dependable and trusted helpmate needs to understand who she is and whose she is to fulfill her role effectively.

A godly helper builds herself up to be effective in her role as called by God. This godly helper asks questions like "God, how would you have me help this man? Show me and teach me to be an effective helper. You formed me for this purpose. What do I need to do to fulfill your purpose for creating me in the first instance?"

This approach to your life and understanding your role will set you apart and above.

A woman who understands her role within the scope of the questions above is preparing herself to be an effective helper as ordained by God in the dynamic of a marriage. It is the lack of this understanding that can destroy destinies and lives. It fuels frustration as purpose has been misplaced. This ultimately resorts to sensually driven decisions and actions with manipulative tendencies.

You are a woman ordained to help. The dexterity of your attributes spans across diverse skills. If you are needed to fight, fight you shall. If you are needed to support, so shall it be. And if you are needed to intercede, you are ready.

> The wise woman builds her house,
> but the foolish pulls it down with her
> hands. (Proverbs 14:1)

What does it mean, "build her house"? To build requires, at the least, understanding and envisioning that which you aspire to achieve. It requires knowledge of the ingredients and materials as well as how these need to be applied to building one's home.

To build a house is deliberate and purposeful. It may sometimes require patience and, most certainly, wisdom. How can she attain wisdom?

Proverbs 19:14 says, "Houses and riches are an inheritance from fathers, but a prudent wife is from the Lord."

If a prudent woman is of the Lord, then a woman who is not prudent, who is she of?

These are the definitions of *prudence* from *Merriam-Webster Dictionary*:

1. the ability to govern and discipline oneself by the use of reason
2. sagacity or shrewdness in the management of affairs
3. skill and good judgement in the use of resources
4. caution or circumspection as to danger or risk

A prudent wife has to know that God is her source and that the ability to effectively fulfill her role as a helpmate is tied to God.

If you don't acknowledge God in your life, you inevitably expose yourself to the enemy and the deception that ensues thereof.

As a prudent woman, your reasoning power is sharpened. You are shrewd in managing affairs and, more importantly, cautious to divert danger or risks from yourself and your house.

I see no reason any woman will reject such virtues. Even if there is doubt in your mind, God can begin the process of teaching and blessing you to build you up; but you have to ask, as stated in James 1:5: "If any of you lacks wisdom, let him ask of God, who gives to all liberally and without reproach, and it will be given to him."

There is a footprint or plan prior to embarking on the laborious task of building anything. This comes in handy when things go south as you can always revert to the template to place you back on course. The template is the Word of God and his intended purpose for you as a helpmate.

A foolish woman has no understanding of her role or her purpose; hence, she inadvertently pulls down her home with her own hands. She has no clarity of vision and lives her life devoid of God's purpose for her, which is to join her husband to fulfill destiny.

> Who can find a [d]virtuous wife? For her worth is far above rubies. The heart of her husband safely trusts her; so he will have no lack of gain. She does him good and not evil all the days of her life. She seeks wool and flax, and willingly works with her hands. She is like the merchant ships, she brings her food from afar. She also rises while it is yet night, and provides food for her household, and a portion for her maidservants. She considers a field and buys it; from her profits she plants a vineyard. She girds herself with strength, and strengthens her arms. She perceives that her merchandise is good, and her lamp does not go out by night. She stretches out her hands to the distaff, and her hand holds the spindle. She

extends her hand to the poor, yes, she reaches out her hands to the needy. She is not afraid of snow for her household, for all her household is clothed with scarlet. She makes tapestry for herself; her clothing is fine linen and purple. Her husband is known in the gates, when he sits among the elders of the land. She makes linen garments and sells them, and supplies sashes for the merchants. Strength and honor are her clothing; she shall rejoice in time to come. She opens her mouth with wisdom, and on her tongue is the law of kindness. She watches over the ways of her household, and does not eat the bread of idleness. Her children rise up and call her blessed; her husband also, and he praises her: "Many daughters have done well, but you excel them all." Charm is deceitful and beauty is passing, but a woman who fears the Lord, she shall be praised. Give her of the fruit of her hands, and let her own works praise her in the gates. (Proverbs 31:10–31)

Verse 10 says, "Who can find a virtuous wife? For her worth is far above rubies."

A virtuous wife is a rare woman, and one needs to seek her out. She is so precious that even rubies and treasures are used as a comparison to advocate for her worth and value. A virtuous wife does not just show up or appear on the scene; there is a phase of preparation and commitment to learn the enriched virtues.

I believe every woman needs to look at her life introspectively, asking questions to understand the work of a virtuous wife. The real question is "Do I meet the benchmark of the virtuous wife?" If the answer is no, then are you prepared to do something about it? It is only prepared people that are going somewhere. You do not wait until you get to the stage to begin preparation; on the contrary, you prepare yourself as though you may be going onto the stage at any time. The stage requires you being a good mother and wife with a focus on purpose.

As I write this, I believe a woman's preparation to be a purpose-driven and God-centered wife plays a vital role in society and humanity. A man who can find a virtuous wife is blessed beyond measure.

There are people who do not have role models and have not been exposed to such virtues. If you fall in that category and desire to imbibe these virtues depicted in the Bible, find yourself a role model. There are several women out there who, by just observing them, you can see how they care for their family, have good work ethic, love their husbands, and possess the dedication and understanding of their role as a pillar of strength for their home. These women are found everywhere; they may be in the church, a family reunion, parties, or even work. The way they talk, go about their business, and express kindness and God–centeredness as well as the priority they place on their family and how they manage their home set them apart. This woman may not always be your mother; she can be your aunt, your cousin, or your friend. But they are out there.

Once you identify them, then you anchor unto them by visiting them periodically or, otherwise, staying connected. These women carry a treasure that will prepare you for life's journey ahead.

Verse 11 says, "The heart of her husband safely trusts her; so he will have no lack of gain."

The heart of her husband is secure in his trust for her that it propels him to do exploits and forge ahead to do better and to prosper.

Verse 12 says, "She does him good and not evil all the days of her life."

A virtuous wife seeks to do her husband good. It is not conditional. Neither is it demanded by her husband. It is an act of her own volition to express and show goodness and not evil to her husband all the days of her life.

I believe any man who does not appreciate a virtuous wife who expresses and conveys good and not evil to her husband is not worthy to be married to her. A man who abuses the virtuous wife is blinded and needs urgent help.

There was once a judge who, unfortunately, had a stroke and was unable to work or perform his duties, but he had a virtuous wife. She cared for him and would feed him herself even though she had servants who could carry out this task. She did this with pride and a sense of love and duty, convinced that it was her responsibility. She also maintained a life and would selectively go to social gatherings. In the middle of enjoying herself, she was mindful of the time and would excuse herself after spending a few hours interacting with other people. She would sometimes explain in preparedness to leave, "I have to go and attend to my husband," leaving everyone speechless.

Had her husband been a foolish man or abusive and also disregarded the virtues of his wife, she could have chosen to ignore him in his current state of vulnerability, but she continued to do good all the days of her life. If he had been abusive, he would have had to live with this guilt forever.

I pray that the eyes of men would be opened to understand the role this excellent and wonderful woman holds in their lives. A virtuous wife really should be cherished.

Verse 13 says, "She seeks wool and flax, and willingly works with her hands".

She is not lazy and works with her hands. She does not go into marriage seeking for what she can get or wondering if she would be financially secure.

I once heard of a woman who said that if she could be married to a very rich sports personality, she and her children would be made for life. Indeed, she married him, and yes, she is worth a lot of money.

I worry about such a mindset as it dilutes the value and worth a virtuous wife can bring to the table. A virtuous woman is not self-centered or calculating, but she understands who she is and who God has called her to be in the dynamic of a marriage.

Verses 15 to 19 say, "She also rises while it is yet night, and provides food for her household, and a portion for her maidservants. She considers a field and buys it; from her profits she plants a vineyard. She girds herself with strength, and strengthens her arms. She perceives that her merchandise is good, and her lamp does not go out by night. She stretches out her hands to the distaff, and her hand holds the spindle."

She is family centered and focused on her goals and objective. She is a determined force who does not relent in her calling. Yet she pursues her God-given focus with determination. Even with the addition of strength and vigor, she is expressively kind and compassionate.

Verses 21 to 28 say,

> She is not afraid of snow for her household, for all her household is clothed with scarlet. She makes tapestry for herself; her clothing is fine linen and purple. Her husband is known in the gates, when he sits among the elders of the land. She makes linen garments and sells them, and supplies sashes for the merchants. Strength and honor are her clothing; she shall rejoice in time to come. She opens her mouth with wisdom, and on her tongue is the law of kindness. She watches over the ways of her household, and does not eat the bread of idleness. Her children rise up and call her blessed; her husband also, and he praises her.

She is forward-thinking while applying herself as a homemaker. In just being who she has been called to be, she adds to her husband's value and status.

Aligning with the virtues of this unique woman of God is an investment that is purpose driven and will ultimately result in rejoicing in the future. Her attributes cannot go unnoticed; hence, her children and husband call her blessed.

She plays out her role not with the self-centered focus of what she can get but, rather, a sacrificial, others-centered focus of what she can give.

Verses 30 to 31 (NKJV), "Charm is deceitful and beauty is passing, but a woman who fears the Lord, she shall be praised. Give her of the fruit of her hands, and let her own works praise her in the gates."

Charm can mislead. The Bible is speaking to the heart of superficial characters that lack the substance or grounding of women whose originality is built on truth and enmeshed in godliness.

A flattering tongue is embroiled in insincerity and can be used to further one's agenda. The deceit of charm is a result of focusing on the wrong qualities. The exercising of charm will usually be applied by forward thinkers; they anchor their lives unto the unassuming, which inevitably and ultimately leads them to disaster. This is more so when the real person's nature is exposed or revealed. The decision of a life partner in the setting of marriage should never be based on charm as there are destiny matters involved.

Beauty soon fades away. We all should be appreciative of beautiful women; and, really, all children of God are beautiful. However, this outward beauty is short-lived as the changes of life set in with age. A decision based on how beautiful a woman looks when adorned with eye-catching materialism is only a mirage without the substance or tensility of a virtuous woman.

So when a man says you are beautiful, it's a wonderful thing to hear, but you should also ask, "What else do you see in me?" You are simply saying there is more to you than just your looks, and you have what it takes to be a woman of substance, as qualified by your virtues.

"But a woman who fears the Lord [reverently worshipping, obeying, serving, and trusting him with awe-filled respect], she shall be praised" (Proverbs 31:30–31 AMP).

A woman who fears the Lord is cognizant of her why, what, and when. She knows her purpose and is instinctively aware about who she is and whose she is. She is focused and determined to please her God at all times.

You will recall that Proverbs 31:10 says, "Who can find a virtuous wife? For her worth is far above rubies."

Who can find this precious woman? She is a defender of that which she has been called to do, a helper, an intercessor, an encourager, a carer, a supporter, and a lover. This woman should be honored and praised.

I know a woman who tenaciously carries out her God-given purpose with a diligence that is resounding. She is a mother of two children. This woman works tirelessly and is well respected in the community where she resides. She has broken the silver lining and continues to prosper in all she does. She is beautiful, intelligent, successful, and wealthy yet humble, and she ensures she gets home to have a meal with her beloved husband. She respects him and loves him dearly while simultaneously caring for her children, who have also called her blessed.

They observe their mother's attributes and how she applies herself to her role as a successful entrepreneur and a virtuous woman. She will spend time after time seeking God and praying while the family is asleep. She is forward thinking in her approach, and her one desire is to please God while fulfilling her God-given destiny.

Chapter 4

The War Has Now Begun

Now the serpent was more cunning than any beast of the field which the Lord God had made. And he said to the woman, "Has God indeed said, 'You shall not eat of every tree of the garden'?" And the woman said to the serpent, "We may eat the fruit of the trees of the garden; but of the fruit of the tree which is in the midst of the garden, God has said, 'You shall not eat it, nor shall you touch it, lest you die.'" Then the serpent said to the woman, "You will not surely die. For God knows that in the day you eat of it your eyes will be opened, and you will be like God, knowing good and evil." So when the woman saw that the tree was good for food, that it was pleasant to the eyes, and a tree desirable to make one wise, she took of its fruit and ate. She also gave to her husband with her, and he ate. Then the eyes of both of them were opened, and they knew that they were naked; and they sewed fig leaves together and made themselves coverings. And they heard the sound of the Lord God walking in the garden in the cool of the day, and Adam and his wife hid themselves from the presence of the Lord God among the trees of the garden. Then the Lord God called to Adam and said to him, "Where are you?" So he said, "I heard Your voice in the garden, and I was afraid because I was naked; and I hid myself." And He said, "Who told you that you were naked? Have you eaten from the tree of which I commanded you that you should not eat?" Then the man said, "The woman whom You gave to be with me, she gave me of the tree, and I ate." And the Lord God said to the woman, "What is this you have done?" (Genesis 3:1–13)

The woman said, "The serpent deceived me, and I ate."

In verse 1, the woman was minding her business when she was approached by the serpent. All he did was pose a question, a question that challenged her very belief and understanding: "Has God said?"

Her accurate response did not deter the serpent, for he was manipulative and deceptive.

The story goes on as the woman ate of the fruit and then offered it to her husband.

In verse 13, "the Lord God said to the woman, 'What is this you have done?' The woman said, 'The serpent deceived me and I ate.'" Yes, the woman was deceived as the serpent was out to take control of the lives of man and woman. Any means to control another person's life against the person's will is simply witchcraft. There was a display of witchcraft by a deceptive spirit whose only agenda was self interest.

The woman saw and experienced something that she had never been exposed to before. She became the first experiential scholar of another way of life, simply deception.

> So the Lord God said to the serpent: "Because you have done this, you are cursed more than all cattle, and more than every beast of the field; on your belly you shall go, and you shall eat dust all the days of your life. *And I will put enmity between you and the woman, and between your seed and her Seed*; he shall bruise your head, and you shall bruise His heel." To the woman He said: "I will greatly multiply your sorrow and your conception; in pain you shall bring forth children; your desire shall be for your husband, and he shall rule over you." Then to Adam He said, "Because you have heeded the voice of your wife, and have eaten from the tree of which I commanded you, saying, 'You shall not eat of it': cursed is the ground for your sake; in toil you shall eat of it all the days of your life. Both thorns and thistles it shall bring forth for you, and you shall eat the herb of the field. In the sweat of your face you shall eat bread

till you return to the ground, for out of it
you were taken; for dust you are, and to
dust you shall return." (Genesis 3:14–19;
emphasis added)

In Genesis 3:14–19, you can follow God's judgement, which started with the serpent (devil), then the woman.

And I will put enmity between you
and the woman, and between your seed
and her Seed; he shall bruise your head,
and you shall bruise His heel. (verse 15)

While God had cursed the serpent, he also placed enmity between the serpent and the woman and their seeds. This is a very important verse as it highlights the perpetuity of enmity between the woman and Satan.

A woman is already at war with the evil one, and this cannot be taken lightly. Every woman needs to understand what they are up against, and this war does not end after she gets married or has children. On the contrary, the war continues and will continue until the end of time.

Remember, God said the enmity is between Satan and the woman as well as his seed and her seed.

This also means that everything that comes out of the woman is subject to attacks from the evil one.

When one is at war, you ought to be watchful, careful, and foresighted. You cannot get too carried away or allow yourself to be distracted. In the field of battle, someone has to keep watch at the tower to sound the alarm when the enemy approaches.

Another person has to be battle ready once the enemy approaches or is in sight. The preparedness for battle is not done when the enemy approaches, for that approach would lead to a resounding defeat. You must be prepared before the day of battle.

Sharpen your weapons and get your armory ready. Fortify your surroundings and have strategies in place to fight a war that is almost inevitable.

If God placed enmity between the evil one and the woman, it would seem wise to adopt God's own strategy for warfare against the devil.

> Put on the whole armor of God, that
> you may be able to stand against the wiles
> of the devil. For we do not wrestle against
> flesh and blood, but against principalities,
> against powers, against the rulers of the
> darkness of this age, against spiritual hosts
> of wickedness in the heavenly places.
> Therefore take up the whole armor of
> God, that you may be able to withstand in
> the evil day, and having done all, to stand.
> (Ephesians 6:11–13)

This bit of Scripture above reads as though to educate us on who we are at war with and what is required to engage in such a battle.

To successfully engage in this battle, you would need to put on the whole armor of God to be well prepared against the cunningness of the devil, as we saw in Genesis 3. This battle is not against flesh and blood but principalities, powers, rulers of the darkness of this age, and spiritual hosts of wickedness in heavenly places.

We have established that every woman is set for battle at various stages, even as a wife and a mother. The preparation starts now and by taking up the armor of God.

At this point, you might be thinking, *Maybe this does not apply to me.* All I will says is, "Keep on living," and then you might painfully say, "I was warned about this."

The wiles of the devil may come in various ways, subtle yet destructive, and it takes a woman who is spiritually alert with insight to engage in this battle and prevail. May I gently remind you that this is not a battle of flesh and blood.

> Stand therefore, having girded your waist with truth, having put on the breastplate of righteousness, and having shod your feet with the preparation of the gospel of peace; above all, taking the shield of faith with which you will be able to quench all the fiery darts of the wicked one. And take the helmet of salvation, and the sword of the Spirit, which is the word of God; praying always with all prayer and supplication in the Spirit, being watchful to this end with all perseverance and supplication for all the saints. (Ephesians 6:14–18)

The armor of God speaks to various anchors that make one battle ready.

"Gird your waist with truth" (*Ephesians 6:14*). What is truth? The Bible explains this quite clearly in John 14:6. Jesus Christ says, "I am the way the truth and the life, no one comes to the father except though me." If Christ is the truth and you put on Christ, you fulfill the Scripture, according to Romans 13:14: "But put on the Lord Jesus Christ, and make no provision for the flesh, to fulfill its lusts." We are reminded that by doing so, we make no provision for the flesh and do not fulfill its lust. This enables the woman to be spiritually-minded.

"Put on the breastplate of righteousness" (*Ephesians 6:14*). Perhaps we should define what *righteousness* means: the quality of being morally right or justifiable. It also means uprightness and goodness.

It appears that being righteous and living one's life in righteousness equips you for a battle that is almost inevitable for every wife.

Proverbs 11:6 says, "The righteousness of the upright will deliver them," while Proverbs 10:2 says, "But righteousness delivers from death."

The breastplate of righteousness will not only deliver you but also deliver you from death. There is a warfare every wife will encounter, but her assurance of survival and deliverance is connected to her righteousness.

I find it interesting that one's character of goodness and being upright translates into one's defense against death.

"Shod your feet with the preparation of the gospel of peace" (*Ephesians 6:15*). This aspect of your armory speaks to your readiness to convey, share, or preach the gospel of peace. This is the teaching of the saving grace of Christ.

Whilst it may seem as an anomaly in the weaponry used for battle, however, it relates to the steadiness and firmness of the feet.

> And how shall they preach unless they are sent? As it is written: "How beautiful are the feet of those who preach the gospel of peace, who bring glad tidings of good things!" (Romans 10:15)

As a woman of virtue who understands her role and assignment, you should be equipped with the gospel of peace and prepared to discharge it to those who need to hear it. It clearly plays a role as it stands to add to you in battle. If you preach peace, it shall inevitably be exuded in your life as it becomes a lifestyle.

"Taking the shield of faith with which you will be able to quench all the fiery darts of the wicked one" (Ephesians 6:16). If you think about what a shield does, it literally protects you from the weapons that are plunged into and thrown at you. That is exactly what your faith would do in this warfare.

Your faith is the expression of God's power in you to overcome. This faith that you carry would achieve and accomplish that which your flesh cannot attain.

> For in it the righteousness of God is revealed from faith to faith; as it is written, "The just shall live by faith." (Romans 1:17)

Your ability to live victoriously and triumph over the attacks of the evil one is predicated on your faith.

> Watch, stand fast in the faith, be
> brave, be strong. (1 Corinthians 16:13)

"Stand fast in the faith"—this appears to sound a warning as though there is a propensity for one to consider giving up, but you are encouraged to remain steadfast in the faith and further encouraged to be brave and strong.

> Be sober, be vigilant; because your
> adversary the devil walks about like a roar-
> ing lion, seeking whom he may devour.
> Resist him, steadfast in the faith, knowing
> that the same sufferings are experienced by
> your brotherhood in the world. (1 Peter 5:
> 8–9)

As a purpose-driven wife, you may periodically need to take inventory of the affairs of your home. You may ask, "What is happening to my husband? He appears anhedonic about our marriage," or notice that your children are displaying attributes or traits that are not aligned with the values of your home. Inexplicable challenges appear to knock at your home repeatedly; hence, 1 Peter 5:8 warns you to be vigilant and sober as *your adversary, the devil,* seeks for opportunities to attack and destroy. But you're implored to resist him and remain steadfast in faith. Your faith is imperative in this fight. More importantly, you need to remain steadfast in it.

I have highlighted "your adversary, the devil" as it is important to have the right perspective and understanding of whom you're engaged in battle with and who he is. He does not like you. He is not your friend. He has no pity on you and does not wait until he feels you're ready to fight or able to fight. He does not care about what you went through a minute ago. *He is your enemy*, woman of God. I cannot emphasize this enough; however, we will come back to this reality in the next chapter.

"Take the helmet of salvation" (Ephesians 6:17). What is salvation? It is the state of being saved or protected from harm. I think questions ought to be asked for you to grasp the depth of the definition.

Who saves you, and who protects you?

Salvation in and of itself begs the reality that we belong to someone. Whose are we?

You must know who you belong to prior to engaging the enemy. You must understand who stands behind you and is for you.

> Then David said to the Philistine, "You come to me with a sword, with a spear, and with a javelin. But I come to you in the name of the Lord of hosts, the God of the armies of Israel, whom you have defied." (1 Samuel 17:45)

In 1 Samuel 17:45, David was clear as crystal that he came in the name of he who is his salvation. He knew whose he was. His salvation was in God.

If God is your salvation, it qualifies you for his defense.

> Truly my soul silently waits for God;
> From Him comes my salvation. (Psalm
> 62:1)

You will notice that your salvation and defense are in God. He is the only one that can defend and protect you.

> The Lord is my rock and my fortress
> and my deliverer; my God, my strength,
> in whom I will trust; my shield and the
> horn of my salvation, my stronghold.
> (Psalm 18:2)

Again, to understand your salvation is to know he who saves you and protects you.

> The Lord is my strength and song,
> and He has become my salvation. (Psalm
> 118:14)

He who can be your strength is also he who is your salvation

> For He says: "In an acceptable time
> I have heard you, and in the day of salva-
> tion I have helped you. Behold, now is the
> accepted time; behold, now is the day of
> salvation." (2 Corinthians 6:2)

He offers you salvation and will help you. If you do not accept this salvation, you cannot access his help. Have you accepted this salvation of the Lord?

If you're unsure or have not, I implore you to do so, for your help awaits you.

> And it shall come to pass that whoever calls on the name of the Lord shall be saved. (Acts 2:21)

> So they said, "Believe on the Lord Jesus Christ, and you will be saved, you and your household." (Acts 16:31)

You need to call on the name of the Lord and believe in him.

"And the sword of the spirit which is the word of God" *(Ephesians 6:17).*

> For the word of God is living and powerful, and sharper than any two-edged sword, piercing even to the division of soul and spirit, and of joints and marrow, and is a discerner of the thoughts and intents of the heart. (Hebrews 4:12)

As I pondered on the verse above, I realized that it is loaded with a lot of information and that the illumination of this revelation is transformational to one's outlook to life.

The Word of God is "living and powerful"; it is alive and has power in it. When you go against the enemy with the Word of God, you are using a powerful offensive weapon.

You need to understand the weapon, its usage, and its application. This clearly requires familiarizing yourself with the Word of God. You do not wait until the day of battle before you learn the usage of the weapon you have at your disposal.

This Word of God is alive. It should flow in you and through you to result in that which it is purposed to achieve. This speaks to Joshua 1:8: "This Book of the Law shall not depart out of thy mouth, but thou shalt meditate therein day and night."

The Word of God is "sharper than any two-edged sword." We all know that a sword is an offensive weapon that is used to either defend someone or attack an encroaching enemy. A sword can have a sharp edge to it, which simply means that only the sharp edge can be lethal; however, a two-edged sword can be very lethal as both sides are sharp, and if swung in any direction, it still has the same effect.

The Bible makes an illustration on the sharpness of the sword. It states that it "[pierces] even to the division of the soul and spirit, and of joints and marrow, and is a discerner of the thoughts and intent of the heart."

If you take the phrase "two edged-sword" metaphorically, it speaks to the introspective nature of the Word of God to the one who imbibes it. It searches the innermost thoughts and intent of the heart.

Are your intentions to use God's Word good? Is your application to use the Word of God utilizing a template of selfishness? Is it self-centered to achieve your own objectives?

Are your intents and thoughts aligned with God's will and purpose?

> Praying always with all prayer and sup-
> plication in the Spirit, being watchful to this
> end with all perseverance and supplication
> for all the saints. (Ephesians 6:18)

Finally, after equipping yourselves with the whole armor of God, you are encouraged to pray always.

Chapter 5

Who Is Your Enemy?

As humans we often find ourselves fighting each other in the marriage dynamic. The question "Who is right or wrong?" or "What about me?" often arises. There is a self-centeredness mentality that is pervasive and ultimately toxic.

Once bitterness and resentment ensue, it becomes very challenging as things begin to spiral down the volcanic hill, following an active eruption. The larva burns and damages everything in its path as at this stage, everything the other person does is met with skepticism.

There is a high rate of divorce and disharmony in the church, and you wonder why? Could it be that people do not understand their roles? A lack of understanding of one's purpose will lead to misplaced focus and priorities.

Could it also be that one person tries to live and abide by Christian virtues, while the other person just takes advantage and resorts to manipulative strategies to control and have their way?

As I spoke to several individuals about the effect of COVID-19 in their homes, some positive feedback was that it made them realize that there were some things that didn't really matter. The arguments and strife suddenly seemed nonsensical in comparison to the impact of COVID-19 on life, and there was an attitude of gratitude that one was alive.

This perspective, forced on people by a pandemic, has helped married couples focus on appreciating and loving each other and not holding on to things as though it was a lifelong battle.

Your enemy, woman of God, is not your husband, children, relatives, or cousins. Your enemy is the devil. The fact that you do not physically see him does not mean he is not working.

You sleep, but he does not. And he seeks out opportunities to destroy that which God has purposed for you.

> Be sober, be vigilant; because your adversary the devil walks about like a roaring lion, seeking whom he may devour.
> (1 Peter 5:8)

Your enemy is the devil. He does not like you, and you cannot befriend him. He is and would always be your enemy, and being in denial would not erase this true fact.

He prowls around, seeking whom he may devour. He tirelessly moves around, seeking cracks and opportunities in the establishment of marriage or your life.

Please understand that he targets the woman's focus and distracts her from that which she was primarily called to do. If he can distract the helper, she cannot offer any help, and the one she ought to be helping is now operating in isolation. Remember, the help from the helper is from God, and it is used to achieve that which God has ordained.

If you call me while I'm at the grocer and ask if I can pick up some fruits for you as you have guest who just arrived from out of town, what you've done is ask for my help because you have a need.

There is no use for a helper if there is no need. The helper helps address the needs that arise and may arise.

I have again touched on the area of the helper as I plan to open up some areas that may be sensitive.

The enemy is after your husband, but he may choose to come through you; hence, you need to be very sensitive and alert to catch on.

The husband was called to work and tend the garden, which means he was given an assignment. To effectively accomplish that assignment, the husband needs to be focused and also in communion with God, who purposed for him to take up this task.

The woman was called to help him and meet needs that contribute to the success of achieving the purposes God has assigned to man.

The woman is required to be more focused on and alert to her God-given purpose to execute her role effectively. She cannot leave any room or accommodate ungodly inter-ference. Hence, Paul, in his letter to Timothy (1 Timothy 2:13–14), says, "The woman was deceived."

Your enemy, the devil, goes after the person who he knows can distract the man from his God-given destiny. The tragedy of this approach is that the destinies of the husband, the children, and the woman are destroyed or distorted.

Every woman needs to understand what the devil is after. He may attempt to use you, woman of God, to attain his own objectives, because he knows, you are a destiny carrier.

There is a serious danger of being lackadaisical on this journey of life. Surely, you have heard of women who started well and, along the journey, started experiencing challenges. The husband who they were called to help became their enemy. I heard of a couple (pastors) who would carry out their duties in church with the diligence required and the optics expected, but when they got home, they would stay in separate rooms. One of the children stated that their mother was the aggressor, as expressed by her behavior. On several occasions, the husband tried to leave the marriage, but the elders of the church would intervene and appeal to him. Unfortunately, he ended up having a stroke and, later, dementia. Though, thankfully, he is well cared for by his children and remains alive. The wife, unfortunately, died shortly after her husband had a stroke. The gravity of this sequel, observed by the children, made one of them state that he was never going to get married. Fortunately, he found a virtuous woman and remains happily married.

Whenever strife or discord, which are both against the fruits of the Spirit, creeps into your home or marriage, you should ideally stop in your tracks to analyze the situation to better ascertain whom you are really fighting against.

It could be the children who are behaving in ways that keep you up at night. Perhaps they are now associating with the wrong peers or indulging in illicit activities that could potentially ruin their lives. What do you do?

Suddenly little Jessica is wearing lipstick or short dresses and staying up late at night. Or could it be that you smell tobacco or liquor on Johnny's clothes, and whenever you confront him, he argues with you and walks off? What do you do?

You understanding your role and purpose in the dynamic of marriage and as a woman will equip you to effectively engage in this battle.

While there is a role for measures to be put in place to address life issues within the context of marriage—such as better communication or being more sensitive—having a listening ear might just be the panacea to understanding and addressing some of the issues that most families encounter.

However, be that as it may, there is also a foresighted approach with underlying tones of an influencer whose only goal is to destroy destinies, steal joy and peace from homes, and kill.

Woman, you have been called and purposed to help him attain the God-given purpose he was made for, not fight him. When you fight him, you fight the wrong enemy and loose a battle that you should be winning.

Have you not heard that enmity has been placed between you and the devil, which will go on till this day? You think he is happy to see you happy and have a peaceful home when you can potentially bruise his head?

A helper is supposed to be trusted, and every man ideally should be reassured in the fact that his helper has his back.

When you as a woman fail to approach your life, especially in the marriage dynamic, as such, you fail to understand what is at stake. Once he distracts you with discord between you and your husband or children, he has crept in to destroy your home, but more importantly, he is after your seed. If he can get you to distract your husband, who then cannot function in the purpose he has been called into, then the devil has succeeded to commence the process of trying to destroy the destiny of your children. He is after your seed. Genesis 3:15 says, "And I will put enmity (open hostility) between you and the woman, and between your seed (offspring) and her Seed; he shall [fatally] bruise your head, and you shall [only] bruise His heel." He is after your seed to secure his own agenda. He is after the future, which is your seed, to diminish purpose and destroy destinies. Do not let him!

The unfortunate issue here is that you were exposed to a deceptive practice from the beginning of time and subsequently manipulated. First Timothy 2: 13–14 says, "For Adam was formed first, then Eve. And Adam was not the one deceived; it was the woman who was deceived and became a sinner."

On that day in the garden, you inadvertently learned a lesson that was tutored by the devil and carried out an action orchestrated by the devil. It's called devilry.

The film *War Room*, by the Kendrick Brothers, is a must-see for every woman of destiny. Please watch this film. It might just change the course of your marriage and your life for the better. Karen Abercrombie, who was a god-sent mentor and guide, understood what it takes to be a purpose-driven woman.

We also see Priscilla Shirer play out her role with passion, not a victim but a warrior, when she understood what she ought to do. She fought the war in her home for her home, understanding that there is a spiritual element and a need to focus on an invisible enemy. And she won the battle.

She shows us that every woman can do this and overcome. Is she talking to you?

Deception is the act of deceiving someone or the state of being deceived by someone.

Manipulation is controlling someone or something to your own advantage, often unfairly or dishonestly.

While deception and manipulation are not specific to any gender, there is a foundational perspective that avails our understanding of these acts.

Anytime the helper, to her own advantage, begins to seek to control he whom she was called to help, she is at risk of delving into realms that have undertones of witchcraft. If this is the case, then you are only operating in a realm that you were never ordained or purposed to be in. A controlling spirit is simply living out a life that is in enmity to godliness and aligned with the attributes of the tutor in the garden, the devil. Don't do it!

You are a woman—a helper called and ordained by God and a warrior made for battle with an invisible enemy to allow destines to be achieved. You can do it. You can win. Just anchor yourself to God, who made you and called you.

Your husband needs you, your children need you, and destinies are at stake but can be realized if you take your rightful place. You need to understand who and whose you are and what you have been called to do. The world needs prayerful women to win this battle. Woman of God, you can do this!

Chapter 6

How Do I Effectively Execute My Role to Be Victorious?

Help is available, and sometimes it might seem over-whelming, as though your home or life is embroiled in a mesh of chaos.

> I will instruct you and teach you in
> the way you should go; I will guide you
> with My eye. (Psalm 32:8)

He who has made you a helper has your back; God won't call you to operate in a role that he knows you cannot handle. You are inherently made for this and born for such a time as this. You cannot give in to your flesh, which reacts to what it sees, but you must and should remain spiritually-minded.

God will teach and instruct you in the way you should go. This will help you approach things from God's own perspective, and he will guide you with his eyes. This in itself is reassuring.

You would also need *wisdom* to navigate the practicalities of dealing with humans, especially your husband and children. Again, he has you covered; read James 1:5: "If any of you lacks wisdom, let him ask of God, who gives to all liberally and without reproach, and it will be given to him."

So wisdom is available to you. All you need to do is ask. I was even more intrigued when I read Proverbs 2:7: "He stores up sound wisdom for the upright."

There is wisdom and sound wisdom, and what qualifies you for sound wisdom is being upright.

Being upright, by definition, is being strictly honorable and honest. It could also mean being righteous.

> God made him who had no sin
> to be sin[a] for us, so that in him we
> might become the righteousness of God.
> (2 Corinthians 5:21)

In the context of our subject, our being righteous exudes from being in Christ; as we are immersed in him, we imbibe his attributes, which reflects in our character.

There is also sound wisdom available to you as you maintain your uprightness in God.

Esther in the Bible is a good example of a woman who understood her purpose, what she was called to do, and her role as a helper for the Jewish people. She was prepared to execute this at the expense of her life. She applied wisdom in her dealings with the king and exhibited this to a standard that is worthy of emulation.

The book of Esther teaches us what it is to be a wife. It illuminates how God orchestrates the affairs of our lives for his own divine purpose while we remain God focused.

> On the seventh day, when the heart of the king was merry with wine, he commanded Mehuman, Biztha, Harbona, Bigtha, Abagtha, Zethar, and Carcas, seven eunuchs who served in the presence of King Ahasuerus, to bring Queen Vashti before the king, wearing her royal crown, in order to show her beauty to the people and the officials, for she was beautiful to behold. But Queen Vashti refused to come at the king's command brought by his eunuchs; therefore the king was furious, and his anger burned within him. (Esther 1:10–12)

In Esther 1:10–12, the king was merry; and all he wanted to do, having shown all his riches, was also show off the queen. He wanted her beauty to be seen and beheld by all. The Bible says she was a beautiful woman.

In verse 12, she refused to come at the king's command, publicly humiliating him, disregarding him and dishonoring him. If she understood order and her purpose, she might have handled it differently.

Perhaps she could have gone as commanded and later, when he was sober, gently and lovingly shared her sadness. Or maybe she could have come up with a future plan where she would be happy to come at a specific time during the celebration and dance with the love of her life or, if you like, the most handsome man in the kingdom.

The concern that women in the kingdom would now see Queen Vashti's action as a template and a standard to despise their husbands concerned the king; hence, she was ejected, rejected, displaced, and replaced. Her beauty could not save her. A decree was sent out to reinforce the king's outlook and decision. Hence, in the book of Esther 1:22, "each man should be master in his own house and speak in the language of his own people"

I am in no way advocating that a woman should be silenced in her own home and serve her lord and master, but I believe every woman can learn how to administer her views and establish her purpose in the dynamic of marriage without leading to being ejected, rejected, and replaced.

> The wise woman builds her house,
> but the foolish pulls it down with her
> hands. (Proverbs 14:1)

Queen Vashti used her own hands to pull down her house; hence, unpleasant consequences occurred. She acted foolishly; one error destroyed her marriage and tore her home apart.

In complete contrast, Esther, who subsequently became queen in Vashti's place, obtained favor and grace in the king's sight, and he loved her.

> And Mordecai told him all that had
> happened to him, and the sum of money
> that Haman had promised to pay into the

king's treasuries to destroy the Jews. He also gave him a copy of the written decree for their destruction, which was given at Shushan, that he might show it to Esther and explain it to her, and that he might command her to go in to the king to make supplication to him and plead before him for her people. So Hathach returned and told Esther the words of Mordecai.

Then Esther spoke to Hathach, and gave him a command for Mordecai: "All the king's servants and the people of the king's provinces know that any man or woman who goes into the inner court to the king, who has not been called, he has but one law: put all to death, except the one to whom the king holds out the golden scepter, that he may live. Yet I myself have not been called to go in to the king these thirty days." So they told Mordecai Esther's words.

And Mordecai told them to answer Esther: "Do not think in your heart that you will escape in the king's palace any more than all the other Jews. For if you remain completely silent at this time, relief and deliverance will arise for the Jews from another place, but you and your father's house will perish. Yet who knows whether you have come to the kingdom for such a time as this?"

> Then Esther told them to reply to Mordecai: "Go, gather all the Jews who are present in Shushan, and fast for me; neither eat nor drink for three days, night or day. My maids and I will fast likewise. And so I will go to the king, which is against the law; and if I perish, I perish!"
>
> So Mordecai went his way and did according to all that Esther commanded him. (Esther 4:7–17)

Haman had planned to destroy the Jews, and word got to Esther through Mordecai. Esther was the cousin of Mordecai, and he had brought her up. Even though she was aware of the dangers, she realized that she had to do what was needful to save her people.

Ultimately, we see a selfless, God-centered woman take a position even though it could potentially cost her, her life. She called for a fast and asked that the Jews do the same. They were to engage in this act of humility while they looked to God.

A woman of purpose cannot win any battle without God's presence and intervention. He made you a helper, and as you practice seeking his face and calling out to him in any situation, you are simply going to the source of your divine calling.

A praying and God-centered woman can change the trajectory in her home as she engages with the divine. This should be a perpetual state of operation in the realm of your calling.

Esther answered, "If it pleases the king, let the king and Haman come today to the banquet that I have prepared for him."

Then the king said, "Bring Haman quickly, that he may do as Esther has said." So the king and Haman went to the banquet that Esther had prepared.

At the banquet of wine the king said to Esther, "What is your petition? It shall be granted you. What is your request, up to half the kingdom? It shall be done!"

Then Esther answered and said, "My petition and request is this: If I have found favor in the sight of the king, and if it pleases the king to grant my petition and fulfill my request, then let the king and Haman come to the banquet which I will prepare for them, and tomorrow I will do as the king has said." (Esther 5:4–8)

In Esther 5:4–8, though she understood what she wanted to achieve, she applied wisdom and invited Haman and the king to a banquet.

At the banquet, the king was ready to grant her petition and even give her half the kingdom. Again, she requested that the king and Haman come to a second banquet due to be held the next day.

Here we already see a display of wisdom and an exhibition of patience even though she knew what she wanted.

I believe that every woman has the ability to wisely and patiently manage the affairs of her home while ensuring that the conduit of communication with God stays intact.

So the king and Haman went to dine with Queen Esther. And on the second day, at the banquet of wine, the king again said to Esther, "What is your petition, Queen Esther? It shall be granted you. And what is your request, up to half the kingdom? It shall be done!"

Then Queen Esther answered and said, "If I have found favor in your sight, O king, and if it pleases the king, let my life be given me at my petition, and my people at my request. For we have been sold, my people and I, to be destroyed, to be killed, and to be annihilated. Had we been sold as male and female slaves, I would have held my tongue, although the enemy could never compensate for the king's loss."

So King Ahasuerus answered and said to Queen Esther, "Who is he, and where is he, who would dare presume in his heart to do such a thing?"

And Esther said, "The adversary and enemy is this wicked Haman!"

So Haman was terrified before the king and queen.

Then the king arose in his wrath from the banquet of wine and went into the palace garden; but Haman stood before Queen Esther, pleading for his life, for he saw that evil was determined against him by the king. When the king returned from the palace garden to the place of the banquet of wine, Haman had fallen across the couch where Esther was. Then the king said, "Will he also assault the queen while I am in the house?"

As the word left the king's mouth, they covered Haman's face. Now Harbonah, one of the eunuchs, said to the king, "Look! The gallows, fifty cubits high, which Haman made for Mordecai, who spoke good on the king's behalf, is standing at the house of Haman."

Then the king said, "Hang him on it!"

So they hanged Haman on the gallows that he had prepared for Mordecai. Then the king's wrath subsided. (Esther 7:1–10)

In Esther 7:1–10, again the king asked what her request was. Ultimately, she revealed Haman's plot, which led to his execution via hanging.

You yourselves write a decree concerning the Jews, as you please, in the king's name, and seal it with the king's signet ring; for whatever is written in the king's name and sealed with the king's signet ring no one can revoke.

So the king's scribes were called at that time, in the third month, which is the month of Sivan, on the twenty-third day; and it was written, according to all that Mordecai commanded, to the Jews, the satraps, the governors, and the princes of the provinces from India to Ethiopia, one hundred and twenty-seven provinces in all, to every province in its own script, to every people in their own language, and to the Jews in their own script and language. And he wrote in the name of King Ahasuerus, sealed it with the king's signet ring, and sent letters by couriers on horseback, riding on royal horses bred from swift steeds.

By these letters the king permitted the Jews who were in every city to gather together and protect their lives—to destroy, kill, and annihilate all the forces of any people or province that would assault them, both little children and women, and to plunder their possessions. (Esther 8:8–11)

Esther approached the king again about her people, the Jews. Ultimately, a decree was passed that allowed them to defend themselves against their enemies, and indeed they did.

Taking a kaleidoscopic view of Esther's life, one cannot help but accept that she had a very eventful life during her early reign in the palace. She acted wisely.

Could it be that you were made for such a time as this, and could it be that the man you married will be lost without your help? Could it be that this man who has never known love is depending on you or that this man who has never had any affection in his life now waits on you? Could it be that you being a helper will enable him to achieve his God-given purpose, which is tied to other lives?

You are a helper for God's divine purpose. Are destinies waiting for you to fulfill your role as such?

Another helpful attribute displayed by Esther is *humility*.

> Remind them to be subject to rulers and authorities, to obey, to be ready for every good work, to speak evil of no one, to be peaceable, gentle, showing all humility to all men. (Titus 3:1–2)

Esther, without a doubt, did subject herself to her husband and king, but more importantly, she displayed humility.

Esther could have taken a different stance as she was now the queen and in the confines of safety of the palace—that the issues or problems that the Jews were about to encounter was no problem of hers and could not touch her. But she didn't.

Esther could have cut off all communication with Mordecai, but she could not forget where she came from and who brought her up in the absence of her parents. And more importantly, though a queen, she was wise enough to relate to all men with humility.

In sharp contrast, Queen Vashti displayed arrogance and publicly humiliated the king. Queen Vashti clearly lacked the ingredient of humility and perhaps was oblivious.

What I also find incredible is that in Esther 1:9, "Queen Vashti also made a feast for the women in the royal palace which belonged to King Ahasuerus."

She made a feast for the other women with the food of the king she disregarded. She clearly had a sense of entitlement and could never imagine that she would soon be dethroned.

How many women, if only they humbled themselves, could have saved their marriages? They pray to God to be married at the singles' prayer meeting one day, yet once married they forget where they started from. They feel entitled and disown their purpose and calling. The risk of arrogance that they may begin to exhibit makes them feel entitled. They are quick to talk back, and they become loud and almost authoritarian in their responses to their husbands. Are you humble?

Another useful component on this journey is your *association*.

> Do not be deceived: "Evil company corrupts good habits." (1 Corinthians 15:33)

If we reflect on the film *War Room*, you will recall that Priscilla Shirer, who acted as a Realtor, now came into contact with the older woman (Karen Abercrombie) who just wanted to sell her house. She was completely oblivious to the fact that her prayer life, marital life, and family life were all about to be changed forever.

She came to see the war room where this old lady had travailed in prayer to win the battle against the unseen enemy. She was challenged not to give up and to fight, hence taking her rightful place.

There were times it seemed like nothing was happening, but she pushed and stayed the course.

We see Esther being brought up and guided by her only living relative, Mordecai. She listened to him and allowed him to speak in her life, especially when it mattered most. She was willing to do what it took to save her people by aligning herself with the wisdom of her mentor.

Another example is in the book of Ruth, where we see Naomi guide this young widow of another tribe to her destiny. Little did Ruth, who was a foreigner, know that she would be named in the genealogy of our Lord and Savior, Jesus Christ.

> Then Naomi her mother-in-law said to her, "My daughter, shall I not seek security for you, that it may be well with you? Now Boaz, whose young women you were with, is he not our relative? In fact, he is winnowing barley tonight at the threshing floor. Therefore wash yourself and anoint yourself, put on your best garment and go down to the threshing floor; but do not make yourself known to the man until he

has finished eating and drinking. Then it shall be, when he lies down, that you shall notice the place where he lies; and you shall go in, uncover his feet, and lie down; and he will tell you what you should do."

And she said to her, "All that you say to me I will do." (Ruth 3:1–5)

Here, in Ruth 3:1–5, we see the positive effect of good mentoring and the guidance of Naomi steering her toward her destiny. Ruth's response in verse 5 is "All that you say to me I will do."

So Boaz took Ruth and she became his wife; and when he went in to her, the Lord gave her conception, and she bore a son. Then the women said to Naomi, "Blessed be the Lord, who has not left you this day without a close relative; and may his name be famous in Israel! And may he be to you a restorer of life and a nourisher of your old age; for your daughter-in-law, who loves you, who is better to you than seven sons, has borne him." Then Naomi took the child and laid him on her bosom, and became a nurse to him. Also the neighbor women gave him a name, saying, "There is a son born to Naomi." And they called his name Obed. He is the father of Jesse, the father of David.

> Now this is the genealogy of Perez:
> Perez begot Hezron; Hezron begot Ram,
> and Ram begot Amminadab; Amminadab
> begot Nahshon, and Nahshon begot
> Salmon; Salmon begot Boaz, and Boaz
> begot Obed; Obed begot Jesse, and Jesse
> begot David. (Ruth 4:13–22)

She married Boaz; and down the lineage, we see David, Jacob, and then Joseph, who married Mary, of whom was born Jesus (who is called the Christ).

I take the view that every woman of destiny should have a godly and tested mentor who is grounded in their faith, and she should know her divine calling as a helper without any iota of doubt. The association with a mentor who can help, guide, and encourage them in the right way (having attained the experiential wisdom as forerunners on this journey of life) is extremely vital.

> The older women likewise, that they
> be reverent in behavior, not slanderers,
> not given to much wine, teachers of good
> things—that they admonish the young
> women to love their husbands, to love
> their children. (Titus 2:3–4)

According to Titus 2:3–4, these virtuous older women are to admonish the young women to love their husbands and children. True love does not look for what it can get but what it can give.

They ought to be homemakers. A homemaker is a person who manages the affairs of her home. She knows what she ought to do to maintain peace, harmony, and love to keep things going while focusing on her calling and relying on her God.

We often hear of marriages failing because a woman has listened to her friends who have advised her to take certain positions on issues that she faces. She stands her ground, and they all appear to be good allies who are always available to offer their support and solidarity.

What remains puzzling is that such friends are ever so dedicated in their homes and are managing their homes and the affairs of their homes. They would not jeopardize their role and marriage at the risk of being ejected, rejected, and replaced.

They do not want to end up being a single mother who only joins the company of these so-called friends only when they are available for her. Neither do they want their children to be exposed to this dynamic. Yet they serve and offer you the advice that they will never entertain. How very sad.

There are good godly friends out there and good godly older women who can admonish younger women in the way of the Lord.

This should challenge you and help you take an introspective look at your life and marriage. There are questions that ought to be asked by every woman of destiny who is looking to be a victorious wife.

Who do you associate yourself with? What do you expose yourself to? Are you exposed to the Word or God, or are you exposed to soaps and films that give you a sense of entitlement? What these exposures do is they satiate and endorse your feelings, but what they fail to do is tell you what the stakes are when it's all over. Who do you allow to speak in your life or marriage? Do you have a trusted mentor, or are you under the guidance of a virtuous woman whose track record shows that she has walked the walk and came out victorious in her life and marriage? Do you have a godly counselor, pastor, or elder you could approach? More importantly, do you have a conduit of communication and a relationship with the one who assigned you and equipped you to assume this role? You need to know your God in spirit and truth!

Your knowledge of God and relationship with him should reflect in your character, actions, and words, evident for all to see. This does not mean just going to church; it also means embodying a deep and loving relationship with God. This relationship is foundational, to say the least.

You know him by spending time in his Word. What does God say about you, your situation, or marriage? What does he expect of you? The manual of life would never be obsolete but always relevant. For those who seek his will and guidance, let the Word of God be your guide.

With an open heart and a willing spirit, he will teach you, instruct you, and guide you with his eyes, as stated in Proverbs 32:18.

Another key to victory is *persistence and patience*. We see this in the film *War Room*. Priscilla, who acted as the Realtor, pushed in prayer. She did not relent even though it was not always easy. You can also appreciate an inner strength and peace as she pressed on. As you reach out to seek him, he will empower and strengthen you.

Esther remained persistent yet patience with fasting and prayers, with the hope that the tide would turn around for the better for her people.

There are attributes that you carry that set you up for victory. God, who sees your selflessness, shall reward you in due time as it shall not go unnoticed.

Selflessness is an attribute and quality that aligns with a woman's role as a helper. A selfless helper is a woman who is completely dedicated and sold out to her role. Ruth was selfless, as seen in Ruth 2:11–13: "And Boaz answered and said to her, 'It has been fully reported to me, all that you have done for your mother-in-law since the death of your husband, and how you have left your father and your mother and the land of your birth, and have come to a people whom you did not know before. The Lord repay your work, and a full reward be given you by the Lord God of Israel, under whose wings you have come for refuge. Then she said, 'Let me find favor in your sight, my lord; for you have comforted me, and have spoken [kindly to your maidservant, though I am not like one of your maidservants.'"

Boaz recognized this attribute and could not help but reward her and pray for her. Verse 12 says, "The Lord repay your work, and a full reward be given you by the Lord God of Israel, under whose wings you have come for refuge."

> Now Boaz said to her at mealtime, "Come here, and eat of the bread, and dip your piece of bread in the vinegar." So she sat beside the reapers, and he passed parched grain to her; and she ate and was satisfied, and kept some back. And when

she rose up to glean, Boaz commanded his young men, saying, "Let her glean even among the sheaves, and do not reproach her. Also let grain from the bundles fall purposely for her; leave it that she may glean, and do not rebuke her." (Ruth 2:14–16)

Here we see Boaz's practical response to her selflessness: he ensured she was fed and had something to drink, and he welcomed her and also ensured she had enough food to carry home.

A selfless helper in her role as a woman of virtue has the attention of God on her matters. Such a helper would go to great lengths to execute their roles, which align with their calling.

Another woman who exhibited selflessness was Rebekah, seen in Genesis 24:12–21.

And he said, "O Lord, God of my master Abraham, please grant me success today, and show lovingkindness (faithfulness) to my master Abraham. Behold, I stand here at the spring of water, and the daughters of the men of the city are coming out to draw water; now let it be that the girl to whom I say, 'Please, let down your jar so that I may [have a] drink,' and she replies, 'Drink, and I will also give your camels water to drink'—may she be the one whom You have selected [as a wife] for Your servant Isaac; and by this I will know that You have shown lovingk-indness (faithfulness) to my master."

Before Eliezer had finished speaking (praying), Rebekah came out with her [water] jar on her shoulder. Rebekah was the daughter of Bethuel the son of Milcah, who was the wife of Abraham's brother Nahor. The girl was very beautiful, a virgin and unmarried; and she went down to the spring and filled her jar and came up. Then the servant ran to meet her, and said, "Please let me drink a little water from your jar." And she said, "Drink, my lord"; and she quickly lowered her jar to her hand, and gave him a drink. When she had given Eliezer a drink, she said, "I will also draw water for your camels until they have finished drinking." So she quickly emptied her jar into the trough, and ran again to the well and drew water for all his camels. Meanwhile, the man stood gazing at Rebekah in [reverent] silence, [waiting] to know if the Lord had made his trip successful or not. (Genesis 24:12–21)

Rebekah's act of selflessness did not go unnoticed as she gave not only Abraham's servant water but also his camels. This selfless helper was chosen to be the bride of Isaac. While she was exhibiting valuable attributes through her act of kindness, little did she know that there was a greater reward awaiting her.

He who finds a wife finds a good
thing, and obtains favor from the Lord.
(Proverbs 18:22)

What qualifies you to be a wife in this context? As mentioned earlier, there are virtues, attributes, and an understanding of the role of the woman that are foundational to this qualification.

The good thing referred to in the verse is the institution of marriage. A woman who understands her God-ordained role as a helper can amalgamate herself to the one who she has been called to help. She understands that she is backed up by the one who called her, God Almighty.

There is a favor from God that results from finding this woman. A wife in this context of marriage is a magnet for God's blessing in her family.

You might say, "I am not this way," "My husband is a bad person," "I came from a broken home, and my neighborhood was rough," "I have failed at this before," "I am not qualified," etc. I say to you, "If you are reading this book and still inhaling oxygen into your lungs, then God is not through with you yet."

I mentioned the unholy partnership that occurred in Genesis when the devil approached and deceived the woman. However, a new partnership occurred to overrule the old. God Almighty partnered with the woman, Mary, who gave birth to our Lord and Savior, Jesus Christ. We were dead (in sin) through the unholy partnership but alive in Christ through the divine partnership. The woman is instrumental to reaching destiny; hence, she was sought after for a partnership arrangement.

If God has not given up on you, why, then, do you give up on yourself?

Do not let your self-destructive thoughts bind you in the shackles of the past and remind you of your failures.

You can have a victorious life, a wonderful marriage, and a glorious future. It begins with a decision.

Talk to God about where you are and what you want, and he shall see you through. Apply yourself with the tools as earlier stated while focused on your God-given purpose, and let's start this journey of purpose.

I really wish not to digress from the topic as this book was strictly written to encourage women out there who may be facing one challenge or the other, women who are unsure about where they are going, women who may have questions about marriage and how they can prepare for this wonderful institution. However, if I may, read Genesis 24:63–64: "Isaac went out to bow down [in prayer] in the field in the [early] evening; he raised his eyes and looked, and camels were coming. Rebekah also raised her eyes and looked, and when she saw Isaac, she dismounted from her camel."

A man whose focus is on God, understands his source, and takes time to seek the face of God is a man who is not perfect but has a scope of whose he is. Rebekah met him while he was in a place of prayer. Are all prayerful men perfect, and would they make good husbands? Not necessarily, but it is a foundational consideration that should not be ignored.

Finally, I wrote this book as I have two young daughters and felt compelled to write this book as a preparatory step and guide for what the future may hold.

Hence, I embarked on the laborious journey to research and understand the role of a woman and wife.

There are many struggling marriages some people have to endure, maintaining a facade and at least portraying a united, happy home. A successful marriage need not be an illusion or fantasy; it can be realized.

I also felt many women could be properly and better equipped for this journey of life.

The excitement and glamour of being in a dynamic of marriage many times supersedes the reality that soon ensues.

Women need this understanding, and they need to realize that the world cannot make it without them.

Woman of God, humanity needs your help.

About the Author

J. Benjamin is a Christian, who is blessed to have been saved and preserved by God. The author was inspired by a quest to understand the woman and her role in marriage, from a biblical perspective.

J. Benjamin is married and blessed with two children.